Date:

To:

As you use this book to study the Word, confess and pray this year, may you become a thousand times more than your fathers."

From:

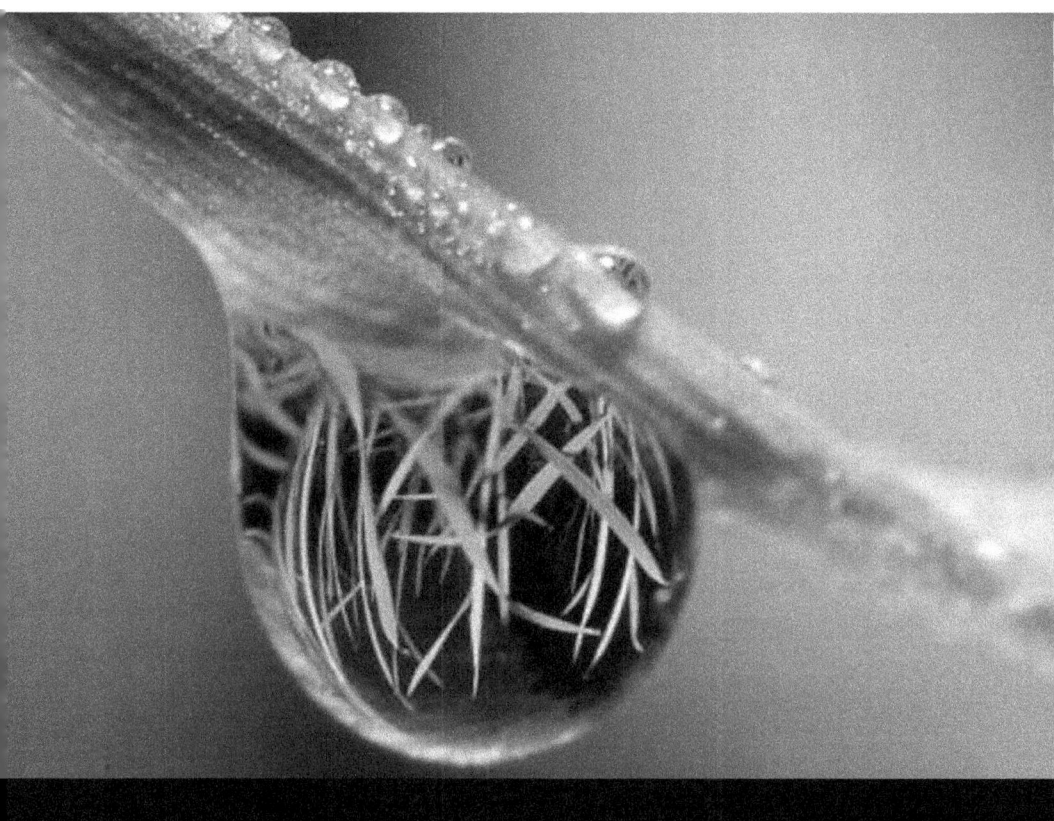

I BELIEVE and CONFESS...

KNOWING AND CONFESSING HIS WORD

Volume 1

ANDY YAWSON

© 2013 Andy Yawson

Published by
Illumination House
P.O. Box DS1277 - Dansoman - Accra - Ghana
Email: illumination_house@yahoo.com

Printed in Ghana
ISBN 978-9988-1-9209-9

All Rights Reserved. No part of this publication may be reproduced, stored in a retrieval system, or be transmitted, in any form, or by any means, mechanical, electronic, photocopying or otherwise without prior written consent of the publisher.

All scriptures taken from the **New King James Version**. Copyright © 1982 by Thomas Nelson, Inc. Used by permission. All rights reserved.

Printed by CreateSpace

TABLE OF CONTENTS

✾ Introduction	7
✾ 1st to 5th January: Uncommon Favour	11
✾ 6th to 12th January: Divine Remembrance	15
✾ 13th to 19th January: Overcoming Limitations	19
✾ 20th to 26th January: Steadfastness	23
✾ 27th January to 2nd February: Nation's Blessing & Peace	25
✾ 3rd to 9th February: Perfected Destiny	29
✾ 10th to 16th February: Victory over Destiny Destroyers	33
✾ 17th to 23rd February: Knowledge of God	37
✾ 24th February to 2nd March: Mighty Manifestations	41
✾ 3rd to 9th March: The Word Of God	45
✾ 10th to 16th March: Honour	49
✾ 17th to 23rd March: Answered Prayer	53
✾ 24th to 30th March: Possibilities and Greater Works	57
✾ 31st March to 6th April: Victory in the Blood	59
✾ 7th to 13th April: Covenant	63
✾ 14th to 20th April: Witness	67
✾ 21st to 27th April: Living Testimony	71
✾ 28th April to 4th May: Power to Prosper	75
✾ 5th to 11th May: Victory Over Deception	79
✾ 12th to 18th May: Fulfilled Promises	83
✾ 19th to 25th May: Divine Empowerment	87

- 26th May to 1st June: Fruits Of The Spirit — 91
- 2nd to 8th June: Boldness and Faith — 93
- 9th to 15th June: Wealth and Riches — 97
- 16th to 22nd June: Exploits — 101
- 23rd to 29th June: Redemption and Reconciliation — 105
- 30th June to 6th July: Harvest — 109
- 7th to 13th July: Soul-winning — 113
- 14th to 20th July: Scattering the enemy — 117
- 21st to 27th July: Anointing For Exploits — 121
- 28th July to 3rd August: Spiritual Authority — 125
- 4th to 10th August: Overcoming Temptation — 129
- 11th to 17th August: Fruit Of Your Labour — 133
- 18th to 24th August: Inheriting The Promises — 135
- 25th to 31st August: Partaking Of The Blessings — 139
- 1st to 7th September: Love — 143
- 8th to 14th September: Power Of God — 147
- 15th to 21st September: Stand up and be Counted — 151
- 22nd to 28th September: Be A Blessing — 155
- 29th September to 5th October: Serving God — 159
- 6th to 12th October: Testimony — 163
- 13th to 19th October: Finishing well — 165
- 20th to 26th October: The Glory Of God — 169
- 27th October to 2nd November: Finding a Life Partner — 173
- 3rd to 9th November: Victory Over Storms — 175
- 10th to 16th November: Destroying Evil Associations — 179
- 17th to 23rd November: Encouragement — 183
- 24th to 30th November: Submission To God — 187
- 1st to 7th December: Success and Prosperity — 189
- 8th to 14th December: Increase and Satisfaction — 103
- 15th to 21st December: Presence of God — 197
- 22nd to 31st December: Thanksgiving — 201

INTRODUCTION

"Sticks and Stones may break my bones but names will never hurt me"

Many are those who have quoted this saying to support their argument that words are virtually powerless and should not be considered to be anymore than they appear to be - mere words.

The Bible, however, takes a different view on this issue and places much value on the role of the tongue in our lives.

It shows us that as much as it is important for us to believe the word of God, the faith that is generated by knowing and believing the word of God cannot remain silent. It ought to speak because the words will put the faith to action.

This is what the scripture has to say on:

I believe and confess...

THE PURPOSE OF THE TONGUE

"For assuredly, I say to you, whoever says to this mountain, 'Be removed and be cast into the sea,' and does not doubt in his heart, but believes that those things he says will be done, he will have whatever he says." **Mark 11:23**

After one has believed, it is the words that puts the faith to action - 'whatever he says'.

THE POWER OF THE TONGUE

"Death and life are in the power of the tongue, and those who love it will eat its fruit." **Proverbs 18:21**

The tongue is so powerful that it can cut both ways and you and I are to choose what we want to use our word for - death or life.

THE PRODUCT OF THE TONGUE

"A man's stomach shall be satisfied from the fruit of his mouth; From the produce of his lips he shall be filled." **Proverbs 18:20**

Your word can actually determine what eventually comes to you. You shall be filled with the produce of your lips.

Having established all these, you will agree with me that it is time we started actively finding out what God's word says about us and confessing it in order to reap the fruit of those words.

This book is intended to assist you in achieving exactly that. Learn at least a scripture a week, make Bible-based confessions and back them up with prayer.

God bless you as you make this your weekly routine!

1st to 5th January
UNCOMMON FAVOUR

SCRIPTURE OF THE WEEK

"But You, O Lord, shall endure forever, and the remembrance of Your name to all generations. You will arise and have mercy on Zion; For the time to favor her, Yes, the set time, has come. For Your servants take pleasure in her stones, and show favor to her dust." **Psalms 102:12-14**

CONFESSION OF THE WEEK

- I believe and confess that as I have stepped into this year, uncommon favour will deliver testimonies into my life.

- I declare that supernatural breakthroughs will be my portion. By my God, I will leap over major challenges and run victoriously through any opposition.

I believe and confess...

- I decree that by the blood of Jesus, healing and health are mine in this year.

- I confess that the Lord will open doors for me as I walk in faith this year.

- In this year, undeniable miracles will break out in my life and I will become a walking testimony in the name of Jesus.

- I believe and confess that I will walk in supernatural provision this year and that I will have sufficiency in all things in Jesus name.

- In this year, I will overcome stagnancy in every area of my life. I confess that I will experience major progress in all aspects of my life.

- I declare that the Lord will elevate me in this season and set me where He has designed for me this year, and nothing shall by any means stop me in Jesus name.

- I confess today, that I will experience financial favour throughout this year and my storehouses shall be overwhelmed by the blessings of God.

- I believe and confess that my spiritual life is transformed this year. My walk with God will grow from strength to strength and glory to glory in the name of Jesus.
- I will be a blessing to many, and many souls will come to know Christ as God uses me to bring them to Christ.
- I declare and decree that I am blessed and highly favoured.

PRAYER POINTS FOR THE WEEK

- Pray that the spirit of excellence will be manifest in all aspects of your business
- Receive the favour of God from all your associates, customers and employees
- Pray for the favour of supernatural addition in everything you do
- Pray that you will continually walk in favour with God and man.
- Pray that at all times the kindness of the Lord will be upon you

I believe and confess...

- Pray that the Lord will bless your life with an overflowing measure of His abundance
- Give God praise because His master-plan for your life exceeds your own dreams.

DIVINE REMEMBRANCE

SCRIPTURE OF THE WEEK

"And let us not grow weary while doing good, for in due season we shall reap if we do not lose heart."

Galatians 6:9

CONFESSION OF THE WEEK

- ✤ I believe and confess that what the Lord has spoken concerning my life will come to pass in Jesus Name.

- ✤ I declare today that the Lord will remember me and step into my personal situation in a unique way.

- ✤ I declare and decree that the doubters and critics will not overcome me as I make my way to my breakthrough.

I believe and confess...

- I confess today that the wind of compromise will not overpower any area of my life. I will not yield to compromise nor fret because of evil doers.

- I declare and decree that those who mock me now will live to see the visitation of the Lord in my life. Those who mock me will witness the divine elevation of my life in Jesus name.

- I pray that the Lord will sustain and strengthen me and I walk into my breakthrough.

- I declare that from today the Lord will remember me in the name of Jesus.

PRAYER POINTS FOR THE WEEK

- Pray that there will be a manifestation of every word of God concerning you in Jesus' name.

- Pray for the grace to stand and be counted for Christ and not compromise no matter what or who comes your way in Jesus' name.

- Pray that the Lord will promote you right in presence of those who mock and despise you in Jesus' name.

- Pray that those who mock you now will come to your celebration as they see the visitation of the Lord in your life.

- Thank God that you are walking into your breakthrough from strength to strength, grace to grace, glory to glory and victory to victory.

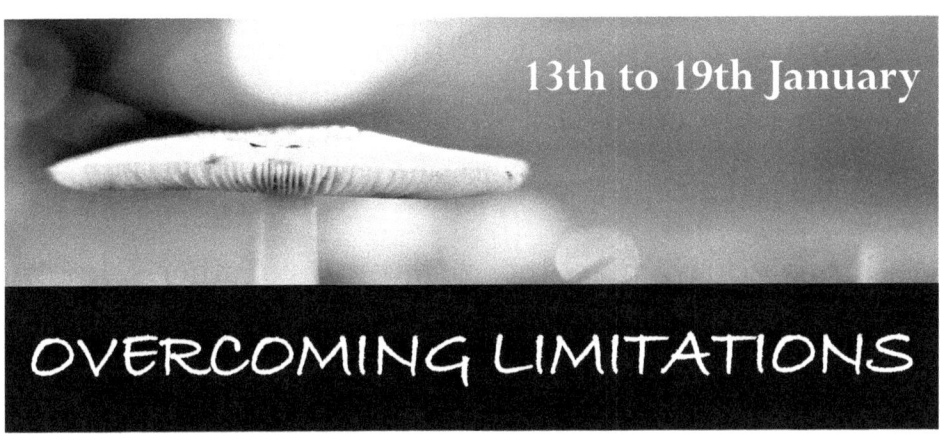

13th to 19th January

OVERCOMING LIMITATIONS

SCRIPTURE OF THE WEEK

"You shall follow what is altogether just, that you may live and inherit the land which the Lord your God is giving you."
Deuteronomy 16:20

CONFESSION OF THE WEEK

- I believe and confess that every chain of limitation drops off my life in the name of Jesus.

- I declare that the power of God will dominate every area of my life.

- As a servant of the Lord, I declare that from today sin will have no dominion over any area of my life. I break out of any addiction or bondage in the name of Jesus.

- I pray today that the Lord will make my spirit

sensitive to His spirit all through my life. I receive divine direction and grace to walk in everything that God has prepared for me in the name of Jesus.

- From today, may the zeal of my Father's house consume me. I confess that I will take territories in the name of Jesus. I declare that God will use me to touch many lives as long as I live.

- God will open double doors in my life and testimonies will meet testimonies in my life. I will walk into unusual fruitfulness in every area of my life.

- I am blessed and highly favoured!

PRAYER POINTS FOR THE WEEK

- In the name of Jesus Christ pray that every chain of limitation is dropping off your life.

- Pray that from today the power of God that raised Christ from the dead will dominate every area of your life in Jesus' name.

- Pray in the name of Jesus that by the power of God that is at work in your life, every hold of bondage or addiction is broken.

✣ Pray for the Lord to order your steps aright to walk in everything He has prepared for you in Jesus' name.

✣ Pray that the Lord will use you to touch lives and empower you to take new territories and recover those yielded to the enemy in Jesus' name.

STEADFASTNESS

SCRIPTURE OF THE WEEK

"But without faith it is impossible to please Him, for he who comes to God must believe that He is, and that He is a rewarder of those who diligently seek Him."

Hebrews 11:6

CONFESSION OF THE WEEK

- ⚘ I believe and confess that the Lord is good and He will continue to be my Provider and Protector.

- ⚘ I declare that as a child of God, I will be consistent in my walk with God. I will never faint nor lose my focus. I reject the spirit of discouragement from my life in the name of Jesus.

- ⚘ I decree that I will not yield to desperation and I will not be distracted from the course where God

I believe and confess...

has destined for me. I will be steadfast and godly fruit will follow my life in the name of Jesus.

- I declare and decree that testimony will meet testimony in my life and I will walk in the season of harvest in my life. I will not miss my reward in the name of Jesus. I shall become a walking testimony.

- I am blessed and highly favoured!

PRAYER POINTS FOR THE WEEK

- Ask the Lord to increase your faith.

- Pray for the grace to be consistent and steadfast in your walk with God and to trust in Him at all times.

- Pray that discouragement will never have a hold over your life in Jesus' name.

- Pray for the grace to be and remain focused and not to be distracted from the course that God has ordained for you.

- Pray that the Lord will reward your trust and faith in Him with fruit and testimony meeting testimony in your life in Jesus' name.

NATION'S BLESSING & PEACE

SCRIPTURE OF THE WEEK

"Blessed is the nation whose God is the Lord, The people He has chosen as His own inheritance." **Psalm 33:12**

CONFESSION OF THE WEEK

- I believe and confess that the Lord God is the God of this nation. I declare and decree that the Lord will reign supreme in the affairs of this nation.

- I confess in the name of Jesus, that peace and tranquillity shall prevail throughout the land.

- I decree that every conspiracy against the peace of this nation shall fail. I declare that every worker (work?) of evil deeds against the nation shall be frustrated in the name of Jesus.

- I confess that the peace and presence of the Lord

shall dominate this country in the name of Jesus. No demonic entity shall find peace or rest in this land anymore in the name of Jesus.

- I reject the advances and manoeuvres of the spirit of death and I uproot every evil seed of violence that the enemy wants to sow amongst us in this land.

- As a child of God, I release the love of God to break out upon this land.

- I declare that this nation is a blessed nation and God's favour shall abound in it.

PRAYER POINTS FOR THE WEEK

- Pray that the Lord will rule and reign supreme in the affairs of this nation.

- As the Lord reigns in this nation, pray that only His will will be done as in heaven in Jesus' name.

- Pray and come against every form of conspiracy, spiritual and physical, against this nation and destroy every work of evil that is meant for the destruction of the nation.

- Release the presence and peace and love of God within our borders in Jesus' name.
- Thank God for His blessing and favour upon this nation.

3rd to 9th February

PERFECTED DESTINY

SCRIPTURE OF THE WEEK

"Being confident of this very thing, that He who has begun a good work in you will complete it until the day of Jesus Christ;" **Philippians 1:6**

CONFESSION OF THE WEEK

- ⚘ I believe and confess that the Lord who has started this good work in my life will bring it to perfect completion in the name of Jesus.

- ⚘ I declare that my God-given dream and destiny will not be aborted.

- ⚘ Everything that God has designed for me shall be made manifest in my life in Jesus' name.

- ⚘ I confess that nothing will distract me from the journey God has set for my life and I refuse to

I believe and confess...

settle for less than what God has intended for my life.

- I declare that I will not yield what God has planned for me to the enemy. Every evil planned by the Devil will come to nothing in Jesus' name.

- No spell of witchcraft, no demonic attack or curse shall be able to stand against me all the days of my life.

- I confess today that as a child of Abraham, I will see, taste and handle the blessing of Abraham in my life.

- I am blessed and highly favoured!

PRAYER POINTS FOR THE WEEK

- Pray that that the Lord will complete and perfect everything that concerns your live in Jesus' name.

- Pray in the name of Jesus that will fulfil your God –given dreams and destiny and nothing shall by any means stop you.

- Secure everything that God has designed for you in the blood of Jesus and pray that this blood that speak better things, will speak their manifestation.

✤ Pray that no spell of witchcraft, demonic attack or curse meant to distract and destroy you will stand in Jesus' name.

✤ Pray that nothing the Lord has planned for you will change hand but you will taste and handle them before every eye in Jesus' name.

10th to 16th February

VICTORY OVER DESTINY DESTROYERS

SCRIPTURE OF THE WEEK

"And Saul also went home to Gibeah; and valiant men went with him, whose hearts God had touched."
1 Samuel 10:26

CONFESSION OF THE WEEK

- ✤ I believe and confess that the Lord is my keeper and my guide. I declare today that everything that God has designed for me will surely be my portion in Jesus' name.

- ✤ I decree today that any association which will cost me my destiny is destroyed in Jesus' name.

- ✤ I declare today that God will deliver me from any 'Delilah' at any stage of my life. I pray that the Lord will expose any hidden traps that will cause

I believe and confess...

me to lose my strength in God in the name of Jesus.

- I declare and decree that from today God will grant me the grace to develop healthy associations and covenants. Men and women, ordained by God, to be a blessing to my life will come from every side.

- I confess that from today God will deliver me from fruitless associations in the name of Jesus. God will surround me with people who will provoke me to good works. I declare that God will send agents of favour into my life.

- I believe and confess that I am blessed and highly favoured!

PRAYER POINTS FOR THE WEEK

- Pray and sever the tie to any known or unknown association that is robbing you of your testimony and costing your destiny in Jesus' name.

- Ask the Lord to restore unto you everything you lost through those associations.

- Pray that the Lord will expose and deliver you from any 'Delilah' and hidden trap that will cause you to stray from God's will for your life.

- Ask the Lord to bring into your life men and women He has ordained to be a blessing to your life.

- Thank God for bringing agents of favour into your life and surrounding you with people who will cause you to become a better person for Him.

KNOWLEDGE OF GOD

SCRIPTURE OF THE WEEK

"But the hour is coming, and now is, when the true worshipers will worship the Father in spirit and truth; for the Father is seeking such to worship Him. God is Spirit, and those who worship Him must worship in spirit and truth."

John 4:23-24

CONFESSION OF THE WEEK

- I believe and confess that the Lord is my strength and He has become my salvation.
- I declare today that as a child of God, I receive grace to grow from strength to strength and from glory to glory. The fruit of the Spirit of God will manifest in every area of my life in the name of Jesus.

I believe and confess...

- I declare and decree that sin will not dominate any area of my life. I establish victory in my private and personal life in the name of Jesus.

- I declare that the grace of God will continue to uphold me as I submit myself to God and His word throughout my life.

- I believe and confess that the Spirit of God will continue to guide me and I will not dash my foot against any obstacle. I will rise higher and higher in my walk with God and nothing can stop or slow me down.

- From today, I declare that I will increase in the knowledge of God and I will do exploits for God wherever I am planted in the name of Jesus.

- I am blessed and highly favoured.

PRAYER POINTS FOR THE WEEK

- Pray in the name of Jesus that the fruit of the Spirit will manifest fully in your life.

- Pray for the grace of God to abound unto you to continually walk in the Spirit and not to gratify the desires of the flesh.

✥ Pray that you will increase in the knowledge of God.

✥ Ask the Lord for the grace to continually and consistently walk and operate in truth and integrity.

✥ Pray that through the knowledge of God you will do exploits in all you do and wherever you go.

MIGHTY MANIFESTATIONS

SCRIPTURE OF THE WEEK

But as it is written: "Eye has not seen, nor ear heard, Nor have entered into the heart of man The things which God has prepared for those who love Him." **1 Corinthians 2:9**

CONFESSION OF THE WEEK

- ҂ I believe and confess that God has purposed mighty manifestations in my life and church this year and they shall come to pass in the name of Jesus.

- ҂ I declare today that I will not be discouraged in any way or by anybody on my way to mighty manifestations in the name of Jesus.

- ҂ I declare and decree that this year, I will give testimonies that will exceed my own expectation. I will give testimonies that will baffle the experts.

I believe and confess...

- I declare that the blessings of God will yield abundant fruit in my life this year and every area of my life shall be fruitful in the name of Jesus.

- I believe and confess that God will restore all the years that the enemy has stolen from life. The joy and celebration I am walking into this month, will exceed any pain of past losses in the name of Jesus.

- From today, I declare that mighty manifestations are mine in every area of my life.

- I am blessed and highly favoured.

PRAYER POINTS FOR THE WEEK

- Pray for a mighty manifestation of that which God has purposed in your life and ministry.

- Pray that no man or woman will be able to stop the manifestation of what God has set to do for you, in you and through you in Jesus' name.

- Pray that this year you shall be far from discouragement and distractions on your way to mighty manifestation.

- Pray that in the name of Jesus Christ you will this

year give testimonies that will exceed expectation and baffle the experts.

✴ Pray that the Lord will restore you on every side in a way that will exceed the pain of past losses in Jesus' name.

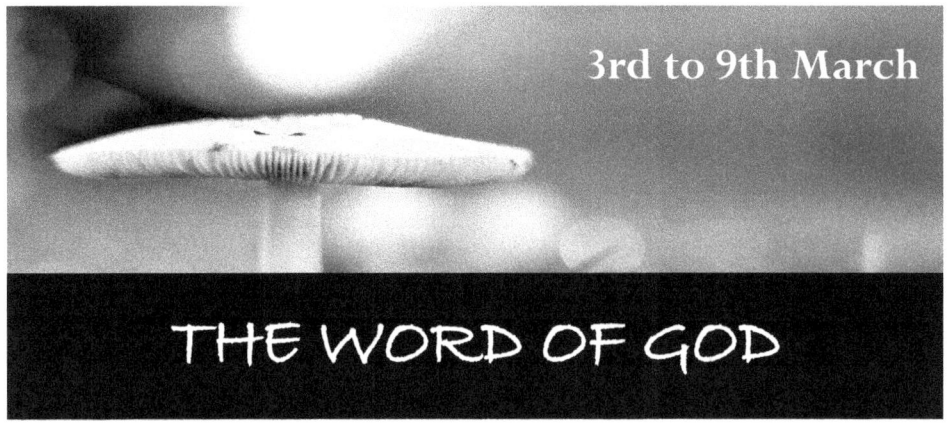

3rd to 9th March

THE WORD OF GOD

SCRIPTURE OF THE WEEK

"So shall My word be that goes forth from My mouth; It shall not return to Me void, But it shall accomplish what I please, And it shall prosper in the thing for which I sent it."

Isaiah 55:11

CONFESSION OF THE WEEK

- ↯ I believe and confess that I have entered the season of Fulfilled Promises; there shall be manifestation of every word that God has spoken into my life.

- ↯ I declare and decree that from today, the word of God that I hear will bear much fruit in my life in the name of Jesus.

- ↯ I command that every attempt of the Devil to steal the word of God from my heart be stopped right

I believe and confess...

now, in the name of Jesus.

- I confess that from today, I begin to take root downwards and bear fruit upwards.

- I declare and decree that the word of God will prosper in every area of my life. I confess that this year my confession shall result in experiences in my life.

- I declare that the will of God shall be imposed on every situation in my life from now onwards in the name of Jesus.

- I believe and confess that I am blessed and highly favoured.

PRAYER POINTS FOR THE WEEK

- Pray that whenever you receive the word of God it will abide and bear fruit in you.

- Pray that the Lord will confirm His word to you with signs and wonders.

- Come against every attempt of the enemy to steal or corrupt the word of God in Jesus' name.

- Pray that the faithful God will cause His word to

I believe and confess...

come to pass in your life.

- Thank God that your hand will handle the things the Word of God promises.

HONOUR

SCRIPTURE OF THE WEEK

"Instead of your shame you shall have double honor, And instead of confusion they shall rejoice in their portion. Therefore in their land they shall possess double; Everlasting joy shall be theirs." **Isaiah 61:7**

CONFESSION OF THE WEEK

- I believe and confess that the Lord is my salvation, my source of strength and my sustainer. I believe that it is He who has given us all things freely to enjoy.

- I declare today that He has ushered me into a new season of my life.

- From today, I exchange my shame for double honour in the name of Jesus.

I believe and confess...

- I declare that instead of confusion, joy unspeakable shall break out in my life and home in the name of Jesus.

- Just as the Lord has shown His goodness and mercies to Abraham, Isaac and Jacob, I declare that everywhere I am planted I shall experience the double in the name of Jesus.

- I declare and decree that instead of tears and frustration, joy and celebration will be my portion in Jesus' name.

- As His blessing pours into my life, I offload every negative burden on my life. As His blessing pours into my life, I receive new fruitful ideas in my life in the name of Jesus.

- I declare that I enter a new season of God's goodness in my life from today.

- I confess that I am a walking testimony from today – touching and reaching lives for Christ everywhere I go. I receive grace to grow from strength to strength and glory to glory.

- I am blessed and highly favoured!

PRAYER POINTS FOR THE WEEK

- Pray in the name of Jesus that from today any thing and anyone that has brought you shame will be frustrated.

- Pray in the name of Jesus that any thing and any one meant to turn your glory to shame will rather bring you double honour.

- Pray that God will disappoint all who have conspired to bring you shame and reproach in Jesus' name.

- Pray that instead of shame God will cause joy and celebration to break out of your life in Jesus' name.

- Pray that God will bring you out of every tight situation and continue to be your shield, glory and lifter up of your head.

17th to 23rd March

ANSWERED PRAYER

SCRIPTURE OF THE WEEK

"Give heed to the voice of my cry, My King and my God, for to You I will pray. My voice You shall hear in the morning, O Lord; In the morning I will direct it to You, and I will look up." **Psalms 5:2-3**

CONFESSION OF THE WEEK

- ✤ I believe and confess that my God is faithful and a prayer-answering God.

- ✤ I declare that as I continue to seek the face of God, I will not abandon my expectation. I believe and confess that the expectation of the righteous shall not be cut off. So it shall be well with me.

- ✤ I declare that God will honour the desire of my prayers that I have presented to Him.

I believe and confess...

- I confess that I am surrounded by testimonies of answered prayer everywhere in my life.

- I receive the spirit of intercession to become a person committed to praying on behalf of many. I confess that God will grant me grace to be able to stand in the gap for many.

- I declare today that for the rest of my life, I will develop great passion for prayer.

- I am blessed and highly favoured!

PRAYER POINTS FOR THE WEEK

- Pray that your expectation this year shall not be cut off but fulfilled to the glory of God.

- Pray that the Lord will honour the desires of the prayers you are presenting to Him as you continue to seek His face.

- Pray that the Lord will surround you this year with testimonies of answered prayer in the name of Jesus.

- Pray for the grace to be able to stand in gap for many no matter your prevailing circumstances in

Jesus' name.

- Pray that for the rest of your life, you will develop a passion and hunger for prayer.

POSSIBILITIES AND GREATER WORKS

SCRIPTURE OF THE WEEK

"Most assuredly, I say to you, he who believes in Me, the works that I do he will do also; and greater works than these he will do, because I go to My Father." **John 14:12**

CONFESSION OF THE WEEK

- I believe and confess that as I set myself to know God's will, His will will dominate all areas of my life. I declare that His will be imposed on every circumstance I find myself in.

- I declare and decree that His power will open all possibilities in my life.

- I declare that in this year all things are possible in Jesus' name.

- As I follow His word, may God fulfil every word

I believe and confess...

He has spoken concerning my life no matter the prevailing circumstances.

- As I continue to develop a personal relationship with Him, may He raise me to do exploits in Him in Jesus' Name.

- This week, I believe and confess that I am blessed and highly favoured!

PRAYER POINTS FOR THE WEEK

- Pray that Lord will always help you know and do His will in every situation.

- Pray in the name of Jesus that any word that is contrary to God's will for your life will not stand.

- Pray that every impossibility in your life will turn to possibility by the power of the Holy Ghost.

- Pray that you will do greater works this year in every sphere of your life.

- Pray that God will fulfil every word spoken concerning you because you believe.

VICTORY IN THE BLOOD

SCRIPTURE OF THE WEEK

"Having wiped out the handwriting of requirements that was against us, which was contrary to us. And He has taken it out of the way, having nailed it to the cross. Having disarmed principalities and powers, He made a public spectacle of them, triumphing over them in it." **Colossians 2:14-15**

CONFESSION OF THE WEEK

- I believe and confess that the Lord Jesus conquered death and resurrected on the third day.

- I declare that the Lord's resurrection has granted me total victory over the demonic powers and principalities of this world.

- By the blood that was shed for me at the Cross of Calvary, every demonic plague and attack will pass

I believe and confess...

over me in Jesus' name.

- I declare and decree that the hold of guilt from sins of the past is broken in Jesus' name. I confess that because of the blood of Jesus, sin will no longer have dominion over me.

- I confess that from today because of the work of Calvary, for my shame I will have double honour.

- I pray that the Lord will cause me to walk in the glory that is restored over my life. I will be strong in Him and do exploits in Jesus' name.

- I am blessed and highly favoured!

PRAYER POINTS FOR THE WEEK

- Pray in the name of Jesus that you will always walk in total victory over the demonic powers and principalities of this world.

- Pray and cancel every evil charge, accusation and demonic plague, and attack with the blood of Jesus.

- Pray that by the blood that was shed for you on Calvary the spirit of premature death, calamity and disaster will pass over you in Jesus' name.

I believe and confess...

- Pray that by the shed blood on Calvary you will have double honour for shame.

- Pray in the name of Jesus that by the shed blood on the cross, the restored glory over your life will manifest.

7th to 13th April

COVENANT

SCRIPTURE OF THE WEEK

"My covenant I will not break, Nor alter the word that has gone out of My lips. Once I have sworn by My holiness; I will not lie to David" **Psalms 89:34-35**

CONFESSION OF THE WEEK

- I believe and confess that the Lord my God is a covenant-keeping God. What He has purposed concerning my life will be done in Jesus name and what He has spoken, He will bring to pass.

- I declare that as a child of the Living God, I receive grace to be covenant-keeper.

- I receive grace to walk in commitment to the covenant I have with God and man. I refuse to be a covenant-breaker in Jesus' name.

I believe and confess...

- I believe and confess that God will give me strength to be a person of my word. In the name of Jesus; I will be known for my faithfulness and consistency.

- From today, I declare that I will be a person who delivers on my promises and I will begin to walk in all the manifestations of the promises of God in my life. I am blessed and highly favoured!

PRAYER POINTS FOR THE WEEK

- Pray that as a child of the covenant keeping God you will enjoy every covenant blessing in Jesus' name.

- Pray for grace to be a covenant keeper like your Father God in Jesus' name.

- Ask the Lord to help you to always be committed to the covenant you have with Him and with your spouse.

- Pray and come against any thing that will cause you to break the covenant you have with God and your spouse.

I believe and confess...

✥ Pray for grace and strength to be a person who delivers on your promises and to be known for your faithfulness and consistency.

14th to 20th April

WITNESS

SCRIPTURE OF THE WEEK

"And they went out and preached everywhere, the Lord working with them and confirming the word through the accompanying signs. Amen." **Mark 16:20**

CONFESSION OF THE WEEK

- I believe and confess that Jesus is my Lord and Saviour and by His blood that was shed for me, I stand cleansed before God.

- I thank God for His mercies that found me and I declare that as a child of God, I will not miss the purpose for which I was chosen.

- From today, I declare that I will not deny my Lord wherever I go. I will be a witness of what the Lord Jesus Christ has done in my life.

I believe and confess...

- I pray that the grace of God will empower me to lead many to Christ. I declare that many will come to know Jesus through my prayer and witness in Jesus' name.

- I declare and decree that I will not live just for myself but from this day onwards, the agenda of the Kingdom of God will be my priority. I will carry the message of what God has done in my life wherever I go in the name of Jesus.

- I declare that I will be a voice for the faith I profess wherever I find myself.

- Signs and wonders will follow me as I declare His word in Jesus' name.

- I am blessed and highly favoured!

PRAYER POINTS FOR THE WEEK

- Pray that you will not be ashamed of the gospel of Christ but rather a faithful witness of what Christ has done in your life.

- Ask the Lord to empower you to lead the unsaved to Christ.

- Pray that the Lord will help you not to live just for yourself but to actively pursue the agenda of the Kingdom of God.

- Pray that without fear or trembling you will be a voice of the faith you profess wherever you find yourself in Jesus' name.

- Pray that whenever and wherever you share the word of God, He will confirm it with signs and wonders in Jesus' name.

LIVING TESTIMONY

SCRIPTURE OF THE WEEK

"The Lord of hosts has sworn, saying, "Surely, as I have thought, so it shall come to pass, and as I have purposed, so it shall stand." **Isaiah 14:24**

CONFESSION OF THE WEEK

- ↳ I believe and confess that the Lord God is my Salvation and my Guide.

- ↳ I confess in the name of Jesus, that I will walk into the manifestation of everything that God has planned for me.

- ↳ I decree that no word that God has released into my life will be stolen, choked or intercepted in any way. Every word that God has for me shall bear fruit in my life in the name of Jesus.

I believe and confess...

- I confess that God will make my life a living testimony. People will see the blessing of God upon my life and will glorify God.

- I reject anything any demonic influences that has caused distraction and delays in my life, in the name of Jesus.

- From now on, I declare that my future will shine brighter and brighter and I will move from glory to glory. God's presence and power will follow me wherever I go in Jesus' name.

- I am blessed and highly favoured!

PRAYER POINTS FOR THE WEEK

- Thank God that He is not a man to lie or a son of man to repent; what He has thought and purposed for you shall stand.

- Pray that you will see the fruition of every word and plan of God for you and nothing shall by any mean steal, chock or intercept it in Jesus' name.

I believe and confess...

- Pray and come against anything and any demonic influence that has caused distraction and delays in your life in Jesus' name.

- Pray that the Lord will make you a living testimony of His goodness and blessing in Jesus' name.

- Pray that your future will shine brighter and brighter and you will move from glory to glory just as God has planned in Jesus' name.

28th April to 4th May

POWER TO PROSPER

SCRIPTURE OF THE WEEK

"Both riches and honor come from You, And You reign over all. In Your hand is power and might; In Your hand it is to make great And to give strength to all." **1 Chronicles 29:12**

CONFESSION OF THE WEEK

- ✤ I believe and confess that the Lord my God is above all and over all. There is none like Him. The earth and the fullness thereof belongs to Him and the silver and the gold are His.

- ✤ I declare that from today God will grant me the heart of a giver that I will not miss opportunities to access Heaven's blessing over my life.

I believe and confess...

- I confess that God will continue to make me a promoter of His kingdom that my resources will never run dry in Jesus' name.

- I declare that my storehouses shall be full to overflowing and the Lord will continue to grant me power to prosper and touch lives in Jesus' name.

- I confess today that as a child of God, my supply shall not be determined by prevailing economic conditions but by the riches of God's glory in Christ Jesus.

- From today, I cease from relying on my own strength alone. I tap into Heaven's supply in the name of Jesus.

- I am blessed and highly favoured!

PRAYER POINTS

- Pray that doors of opportunities to access Heaven's blessing will open over your life.

- Pray that the Lord will grant you a heart of a giver, that greed and selfishness will be far from you in Jesus' name.

- Pray that the Lord will make you and your household promoters of His kingdom in Jesus' name.

- Pray that as you promote the kingdom of God, He will cause your storehouse to be full to overflowing in Jesus' name.

- Pray that the Lord will continue to grant you power to prosper and touch lives in Jesus' name.

VICTORY OVER DECEPTION

SCRIPTURE OF THE WEEK

"Our soul has escaped as a bird from the snare of the fowlers; the snare is broken, and we have escaped. Our help is in the name of the Lord, Who made heaven and earth."

Psalms 124:7-8

CONFESSION OF THE WEEK

- I believe and confess that the Lord is my Keeper and my Guide. The Lord will order my steps all the days of my life.

- I pray today that the Lord will give me the grace to incline my heart to divine wisdom and instruction.

- I pray today that the Lord will give me a teachable spirit and godly patience to seek and wait for His will to manifest in my life.

I believe and confess...

- I declare and decree that every hold of deception set against me is broken in Jesus' name. The pit of deception that the enemy has dug for me will trap those who dug it in Jesus' name.

- I declare and decree that from today the spirit of discernment will go with me in all decisions that I make.

- I confess that I will not be a victim to deception in my walk with God but rather a weapon in the hands of the Almighty to lead people out of deception.

- I am a child of Light and God's light will continually guide me.

- I believe and confess that I am blessed and highly favoured!

PRAYER POINTS FOR THE WEEK

- Pray that for the rest of your life the Lord will be your keeper and guide.

- Pray that the Lord will help you not to fall into any snare of the enemy in Jesus' name.

I believe and confess...

- Pray that the snares the enemy has set for you will trap those who set them in Jesus' name.

- Ask the Lord to give you the spirit of discernment that you will be able to discern good from evil.

- Pray that as you walk with the Lord He will make you a weapon in His hand to lead people out deception and every snare of the enemy.

FULFILLED PROMISES

SCRIPTURE OF THE WEEK

"God is not a man, that He should lie, Nor a son of man, that He should repent. Has He said, and will He not do? Or has He spoken, and will He not make it good?

Numbers 23:19

CONFESSION OF THE WEEK

- I believe and confess that my God is a faithful God and He cannot lie.
- I declare that everything that the Lord God has said about me shall come to pass in Jesus' name.
- I confess today that no opposition, no frustration, no delay shall rob me of what God has destined for me.

I believe and confess...

- ✤ I declare today that, just as Abraham, I rise above every negative report and situations that appear hopeless to men.

- ✤ I confess today that the healing from heaven, the open doors from heaven, the blessing from heaven is mine in Jesus' name.

- ✤ I declare that from today the will of God in heaven shall be imposed on my situation here on earth in the name of Jesus. Every limitation and demonic opposition is broken in Jesus' name.

- ✤ I am blessed and highly favoured!

PRAYER POINTS FOR THE WEEK

- ✤ Pray for grace to hold on unto every word He has given you.

- ✤ Pray that there will be a manifestation of everything the Lord has said about you in Jesus' name.

- ✤ Pray in the name of Jesus that no amount of conspiracy and opposition will rob you of what God destined for you.

I believe and confess...

- Pray for the grace and strength to rise above every negative report and circumstances.
- Thank God for His will alone will be done in your life.

19th to 25th May

DIVINE EMPOWERMENT

SCRIPTURE OF THE WEEK

"Declaring the end from the beginning, And from ancient times things that are not yet done, saying, 'My counsel shall stand, And I will do all My pleasure,' Calling a bird of prey from the east, The man who executes My counsel, from a far country. Indeed I have spoken it; I will also bring it to pass. I have purposed it; I will also do it." **Isaiah 46:10-11**

CONFESSION OF THE WEEK

- I believe and confess that the counsel of the Lord shall stand in every area of my life in the name of Jesus.

- I declare and decree that no battle or delay will outlast the mercies of God in my life.

I believe and confess...

- I confess today that no storm will break my focus on God's word concerning my life. No mountain shall overshadow God's plan for my life.

- I decree that what God has purposed will be my testimony and what He has spoken will manifest in my life.

- I declare and decree that God will go to great lengths to fulfil His promises in my life this year.

- In this year, I will exceed every demonic boundary and overwhelm every limitation in my life in Jesus' name.

- I believe and confess that I am blessed and highly favoured!

PRAYER POINTS FOR THE WEEK

- Thank God that only His counsel shall stand in every area of my life.

- Destroy every mountain that is trying to overshadow God's plan for your life.

- Pray that there will be a manifestation in your life of what God has purposed and spoken in Jesus' name.

- Pray that the Lord will arise on your behalf and cause His promises to be fulfilled in your life in Jesus' name.

- Pray that the Lord will bring you help needed from afar and near to exceed every demonic boundary and overwhelm every limitation in Jesus' name.

FRUITS OF THE SPIRIT

SCRIPTURE OF THE WEEK

"But the fruit of the Spirit is love, joy, peace, longsuffering, kindness, goodness, faithfulness, gentleness, self-control. Against such there is no law." **Galatians 5:22-23**

CONFESSION OF THE WEEK

- I believe and confess that the fruit of the Spirit will manifest in my life.

- I confess that the love of God will be shed abroad in my heart in the name of Jesus. I declare that joy and peace will be evident in my life from this day onwards.

- I confess that longsuffering and kindness will be seen in my life and goodness and faithfulness will be my portion.

I believe and confess...

- I will carry the testimony of being a good and faithful person in the name of Jesus.
- I declare and decree that the spirit of gentleness will rest on my life and I will exercise self-control in every area of my life.
- I am blessed and highly favoured!

PRAYER POINTS FOR THE WEEK

- Ask the Lord to give you His unspeakable joy that gives strength in Jesus' name.
- Pray that the peace of God that surpasses all understanding will keep and guard your mind and heart at all times.
- Pray that the Lord will give you the spirit of meekness and humility and the grace to submit to authority.
- Pray that the Lord will help you exhibit a worthy example of the lifestyle of His kingdom in Jesus' name.
- Thank God that you will manifest all the fruits of the Spirit in your life.

BOLDNESS AND FAITH

SCRIPTURE OF THE WEEK

"By faith Noah, being divinely warned of things not yet seen, moved with godly fear, prepared an ark for the saving of his household, by which he condemned the world and became heir of the righteousness which is according to faith."

Hebrews 11:7

CONFESSION OF THE WEEK

- ↳ I believe and confess that I serve a Living God, the Maker of Heaven and Earth.

- ↳ I decree that any tendency to stay unresponsive to God's word is broken over my life in the name of Jesus.

- ↳ I declare and decree as a child of God, that I am no longer bound by the fear of the unknown in the name of Jesus. I confess that I receive boldness to step out by faith on God's word concerning my life.

- I confess that God has granted me a heart that will place great value on God's word and His word will bear great fruit in my life, in Jesus' name.

- I believe and confess that boldness to take risk in obeying God's word has come upon me now, in the name of Jesus.

- From today, I will pay the price to step out and obey God's word and I will reap a mighty harvest in the name of Jesus.

- I believe and confess that I am blessed and highly favoured!

PRAYER POINTS FOR THE WEEK

- Pray in the name of Jesus and bind the spirit of fear that makes you unresponsive to the word of God.

- Pray for grace to always move and operate by faith and not by sight.

I believe and confess...

- Take authority and break the grip of the fear of the unknown over your life in Jesus' name.

- Pray and come against anything that is hindering your faith in Jesus' name.

- Thank God for endowing you with boldness to take risk in obeying God's word.

9th to 15th June

WEALTH AND RICHES

SCRIPTURE OF THE WEEK

"His descendants will be mighty on earth; the generation of the upright will be blessed. Wealth and riches will be in his house, And his righteousness endures forever."

Psalms 112:2-3

CONFESSION OF THE WEEK

- I believe and confess that the Lord is my source of supply. He continues to bless me according to His riches in glory in Christ Jesus.
- He has appointed for me to walk in abundance and has given me the power to get wealth.
- I declare and decree that from today, I sever any link with poverty in my life in Jesus' name. I will no longer labour and not see harvest.

I believe and confess...

- I believe and confess that as I diligently seek the Lord and obey His word, wealth and riches shall be in my house. I will not only prosper but I will continue to prosper until I am very prosperous.

- I destroy the hold of a poverty mentality over my mind in Jesus' name. I reject the tendency to glorify poverty in my life.

- I receive the grace and anointing to use my wealth to influence communities for Christ. I receive the grace to use my wealth to touch lives and be a blessing.

- I receive grace to use my wealth to impact my generation.

- In this year, I declare that as I continue to honour God in my life, my barns shall be filled with plenty and my vats shall overflow in the name of Jesus.

- I declare that I will continue to do good to those who are of the household of faith in Jesus' name.

- I am blessed and highly favoured!

PRAYER POINTS FOR THE WEEK

- Pray and sever any link with poverty in your life in Jesus' name.

- Pray that you will no longer labour and not see harvest.

- Pray in the name of Jesus that as you diligently seek the Lord and obey His word, wealth and riches shall never depart from your house.

- Pray that the Lord will continue to prosper you and your children until you become very prosperous.

- Pray for the grace to continue to do good to those who are of the household of faith in Jesus' name.

16th to 22nd June

EXPLOITS

SCRIPTURE OF THE WEEK

"Then you shall know that I am in the midst of Israel: I am the Lord your God and there is no other. My people shall never be put to shame." **Joel 2:27**

CONFESSION OF THE WEEK

- I believe and confess that as I follow His word, God will fulfil every word He has spoken concerning my life no matter the prevailing circumstances.
- He will cause me to go beyond every limitation in order to experience what
- He has designed for me.
- As I continue to develop a personal relationship with Him, He will raise me to do exploits in Him in Jesus' name.

I believe and confess...

- As a servant of the Lord, I declare that from today signs and wonders will follow every area of my life. I will bear great fruit in my spiritual life and I step into the overflow, in Jesus' name.

- From today, I declare and decree that I shift from :-
  - An admirer of Christ to a disciple of Christ
  - Being blessed to being a blessing
  - A receiver to a giver
  - Being encouraged to becoming an encourager
  - Being a complainer to being a promoter of God's kingdom
  - Being an analyst to becoming an intercessor
  - A church member to a true worshipper
  - An observer of God's miracles to a miracle-worker for God

- This week, I believe and confess that I am blessed and highly favoured!

PRAYER POINTS FOR THE WEEK

- Pray and destroy anything that is trying to limit and prevent you from experiencing what God has designed for you in Jesus' name.

- Pray that the Lord will raise you to do exploits as you continue to develop a personal relationship with Him in Jesus' name.

- Pray that signs and wonders will manifest in every area of your life in Jesus' name.

- Pray that the Lord will cause you to bear great fruit in your spiritual life and step into the overflow, in Jesus' Name.

- Thank God for making you a true worshiper in Jesus' name.

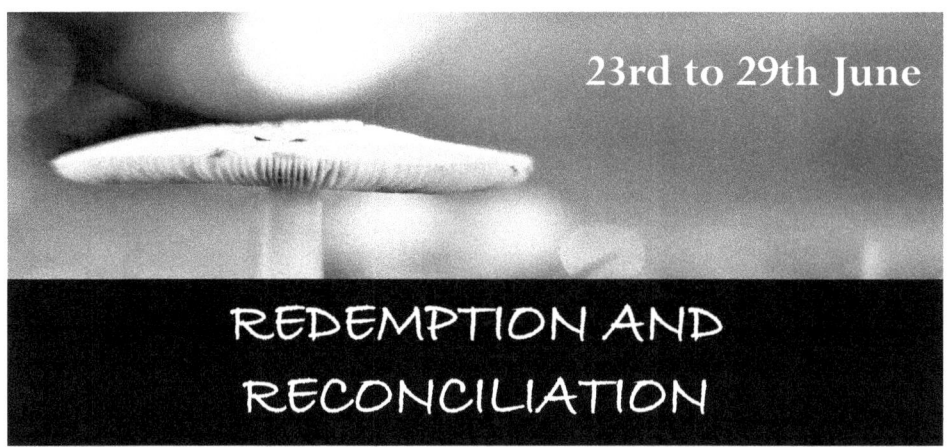

23rd to 29th June

REDEMPTION AND RECONCILIATION

SCRIPTURE OF THE WEEK

"What shall I render to the Lord For all His benefits toward me? I will take up the cup of salvation, and call upon the name of the Lord." **Psalms 116:12-13**

CONFESSION OF THE WEEK

- I believe and confess that the Lord has redeemed me from the curse of the law and reconciled me to Himself.

- I declare and decree that I receive fresh anointing to make full proof of my ministry as a minister of reconciliation.

- I declare that from today I offer myself, my time, my money, my talents and abilities to serve and honour God and see lives reconciled to Him.

I believe and confess...

- I break any hold of lukewarmness over my spiritual life and destroy any spiritual slumber that makes me unwilling to actively serve God in Jesus' name.

- I confess that from today I will stand up and be counted amongst those who are actively living for Christ.

- I am blessed and highly favoured!

PRAYER POINTS FOR THE WEEK

- Pray in the name of Jesus that no curse against you will stand because Christ has redeemed you from the curse of the law and reconciled you to Himself.

- Pray for fresh anointing to make full proof of your ministry as a minister of reconciliation.

- Ask the Lord to give you grace to be able to offer yourself, your time, your money, your talents and abilities to serve and honor God and see lives reconciled to Him.

- Pray and break any hold of lukewarmness over your spiritual life and destroy any spiritual slumber

I believe and confess...

that makes people unwilling to actively serve God in Jesus name.

✣ Pray for grace that will make you from today stand up and be counted amongst those who are actively living for Christ.

30th June to 6th July

HARVEST

SCRIPTURE OF THE WEEK

"Do you not say, 'There are still four months and then comes the harvest'? Behold, I say to you, lift up your eyes and look at the fields, for they are already white for harvest!"

John 4:35

CONFESSION OF THE WEEK

- I believe and confess that I serve the Lord of the harvest. I declare today that I will not miss the harvest in any area of my life in the name of Jesus.

- I declare that as a child of the Living God, that anything that is blocking or delaying my harvest is destroyed in Jesus' name.

- I receive grace to harvest souls for the kingdom of God in the name of Jesus. I confess that the Lord

I believe and confess...

will use me to lead people to the knowledge of the Lord Jesus Christ.

✥ I believe and confess, that the harvest that God has already prepared for my life will be made manifest in Jesus' name.

✥ I declare that from today, fruit will follow every area of my life. My spiritual life will see fruitfulness in the name of Jesus. My family life will see fruit in the name of Jesus. The works of my hands will see fruit in the name of Jesus.

✥ What God assigned for my life will not be left undone in the name of Jesus.

✥ I am blessed and highly favoured!

PRAYER POINTS FOR THE WEEK

✥ Pray that the Lord will help you not to miss the harvest in any area of your life in the name of Jesus.

✥ Pray and destroy anything that is blocking or delaying your harvest in Jesus' name.

✥ Pray for grace to harvest souls for the kingdom of

God in the name of Jesus.

✥ Ask the Lord will use you to lead people to the knowledge of the Lord Jesus Christ.

✥ Pray that the harvest that God has already prepared for your life, family, business and ministry will be made manifest in Jesus' name.

7th to 13th July

SOUL-WINNING

SCRIPTURE OF THE WEEK

"Also I heard the voice of the Lord, saying: "Whom shall I send, and who will go for Us?" Then I said, "Here am I! Send me."" **Isaiah 6:8**

CONFESSION OF THE WEEK

- ⚘ I believe and confess that Jesus is my Lord and personal Saviour. God paid the ultimate price for my salvation and I am grateful to God for that.

- ⚘ I declare that as a child of God, I have come to Him and I will avail myself to be trained and go out carrying the gospel to others.

- ⚘ From today, I will make myself available for the pursuing of the kingdom agenda. I will make myself available to be used of God to win souls for

I believe and confess...

Christ.

- I will not just stay in His House, I will go and preach His word because He has sent me.

- I declare and decree that I, from today, will be an active promoter of the kingdom of God wherever I go. My financial resources will send the gospel to places I have never been.

- I declare that signs and wonders will follow me as I win souls for Christ.

- I am blessed and highly favoured!

PRAYER POINTS FOR THE WEEK

- Pray for grace to humble and avail yourself to be trained and go out carrying the gospel to others in Jesus' name.

- Pray that regardless of the prevailing circumstance you will make yourself available for the pursuing of the kingdom agenda.

- Pray that the Lord will perform signs and wonders by your hands as you make yourself available to be used of God to win souls for Christ.

- Pray for boldness not to just stay in the House of the Lord but to go and preach His word because He has sent you.

- Pray that the Lord will endow you financially and spiritually from today to be an active promoter of the kingdom of God wherever you go.

14th to 20th July

SCATTERING THE ENEMY

SCRIPTURE OF THE WEEK

"Let God arise, Let His enemies be scattered; Let those also who hate Him flee before Him." **Psalms 68:1**

CONFESSION OF THE WEEK

- I believe and confess that the Lord God is my rock, my fortress and my deliverer.

- I confess in the name of Jesus, that though I walk in the valley of the shadow of death, the Lord will be with me all the way and I will come out victorious.

- I declare that the Lord is my shield and no fiery dart of the Devil set against me shall find its target. In the name of Jesus, I cancel the effect of all spells, vows and curses set against me.

- I decree that those who have assembled against me

I believe and confess...

shall fall for my sake in name of Jesus.

- As a child of God, I send confusion to the camp of the enemy and declare that the armies of God will scatter the work of the Devil against any area of my life.

- I confess today that the Lord will build His church and the gates of Hell shall not prevail against it, in Jesus' name.

- I am blessed and highly favoured!

PRAYER POINTS FOR THE WEEK

- Pray that though you walk in the valley of the shadow of death, the Lord will continually be with you all the way and you will come out victorious.

- Pray that no fiery dart of the Devil set against you shall find its target in the name of Jesus.

- Pray and cancel the effect of all spells, vows and curses set against you in Jesus' name.

- Pray that those who have conspired and assembled against you shall fall for your sake in the name of Jesus.

✥ Pray and send confusion to the camp of the enemy and declare that the armies of God will scatter the work of the Devil against any area of your life and family.

21st to 27th July
ANOINTING FOR EXPLOITS

SCRIPTURE OF THE WEEK

"Then Samuel took the horn of oil and anointed him in the midst of his brothers; and the Spirit of the Lord came upon David from that day forward. So Samuel arose and went to Ramah." **1 Samuel 16:13**

CONFESSION OF THE WEEK

- I believe and confess that I have received an outpouring of the Holy Spirit upon my life in Jesus' name.

- I declare that this infilling has given me divine insight. My eyes are opened to see things from God's perspective in the name of Jesus. I begin to see the supernatural in Jesus' name.

- I confess that I am empowered for every

assignment that God has given me and I declare that from today I will be fruitful in winning souls for Christ in my personal life in Jesus' name.

- I receive grace to be a soul-winner.
- I declare that from today I receive grace to do the unusual. I receive grace to do what is beyond my natural ability in Jesus' name.
- From today, I confess that supernatural results will follow all my endeavours in Jesus' name. God will bring me harvest that far outweighs my natural effort and labour in the name of Jesus.
- I am blessed and highly favoured!

PRAYER POINTS FOR THE WEEK

- Ask the Lord for a fresh outpouring of the Holy Spirit upon your life in Jesus' name.
- Pray that the infilling of the Holy Spirit will give you divine insight and that your eyes will open to see things from God's perspective in Jesus' name.
- I begin to see the supernatural in Jesus' name.
- Pray that the Lord will empower you for every

assignment that He has given you.

- Pray for grace to do what is beyond your natural ability and thank God that supernatural results will follow all your endeavours in Jesus' name.

SPIRITUAL AUTHORITY

SCRIPTURE OF THE WEEK

"By a prophet the Lord brought Israel out of Egypt, and by a prophet he was preserved." **Hosea 12:13**

CONFESSION OF THE WEEK

- I believe and confess that the Lord will cause me to enter the destiny that He has prepared for me.

- I pray today that the Lord will continue to bless and anoint those He has set in spiritual authority over my life, to walk in the centre of the will of God.

- I pray that the Lord will continue to put fresh word in the mouth of those that speak God's word into my life.

- I pray that the Lord will cause divine wisdom to be

I believe and confess...

the portion of those who lead me in the things of God. I declare and decree that the Lord will grant me a humble and teachable spirit in Jesus' name.

- Rebellion and dishonour will not be my portion in Jesus' name.

- I declare and decree that from today I will not despise the house of God. I declare and decree that I will not despise those God has put in spiritual authority over my life.

- I declare and decree that I will not dishonour the family of God in the name of Jesus. I am thankful for the house where God has planted me.

- I am blessed and highly favoured!

PRAYER POINTS FOR THE WEEK

- Pray that the Lord will cause you to enter the destiny that He has prepared for you.

- Pray today that the Lord will continue to bless and anoint those He has set in spiritual authority over your life, to walk in the centre of His will.

- Pray that the Lord will continue to put fresh word

in the mouth of those that speak His word into your life.

✤ Pray that rebellion and dishonour will not be your portion and you will not despise those God has put in spiritual authority over your life in Jesus' name.

✤ Thank God for the house where He has planted you.

OVERCOMING TEMPTATION

SCRIPTURE OF THE WEEK

"So all the days of Enoch were three hundred and sixty-five years. And Enoch walked with God; and he was not, for God took him." **Genesis 5:23-24**

CONFESSION OF THE WEEK

- I believe and confess that I serve a great God and the Holy One.

- I declare that by the blood of Jesus that was shed for me, I stand cleansed before the Almighty God. In Him, I live and move and have my being and my righteousness is of Him.

- I confess that by His grace and mercy, I walk in righteousness and in obedience to His word all through my life.

I believe and confess...

- I break the hold of compromise over every area of my life. I receive boldness and strength to overcome any temptation to compromise.

- I receive favour that will cause me to excel whilst upholding my conviction in God.

- I confess today that my life of obedience will attract unusual favour wherever I go. I will walk into testimonies that will go beyond the understanding of the natural man. My seed shall attract heavenly harvest in the name of Jesus.

- I am blessed and highly favoured!

PRAYER POINTS FOR THE WEEK

- Pray for grace to continually walk in righteousness and in obedience to the word of God all through your life.

- Pray and destroy the grip of compromise over every area of your life.

- Ask the Lord for boldness and strength to overcome any temptation to compromise in Jesus' name.

✤ Pray for grace and favour that will cause you to excel whilst upholding your conviction in God.

✤ Thank God that He is causing you to attract unusual favour wherever you go as you live a life of obedience.

FRUIT OF YOUR LABOUR

SCRIPTURE OF THE WEEK

"Therefore, my beloved brethren, be steadfast, immovable, always abounding in the work of the Lord, knowing that your labor is not in vain in the Lord." **1 Corinthians 15:58**

CONFESSION OF THE WEEK

- I believe and confess that every word that God sends into my life this year will bear much fruit. I declare that I will not be just a hearer of God's word but a doer in Jesus' name.

- As a child of the Most High, I refuse to give up on the blessing that God has in store for me. I declare and decree that I will not miss the timing of God in my life.

- I will not miss the package of heaven meant for my life. I confess that fruit will follow every seed I sow.

I believe and confess...

The seed of the past will speak for me now in the name of Jesus.

- I declare that my labour of love will not go unrewarded.
- I believe and confess that I am blessed and highly favoured!

PRAYER POINTS FOR THE WEEK

- Pray in the name of Jesus that you will see the fruition of every word that God sends into your life.
- Pray for the grace not to be just to be a hearer of God's word but a doer in Jesus' Name.
- Pray for the grace not to go ahead of God and also not to miss His timing in your life.
- Pray that you will not give up on the blessing that God has in store for you this year.
- Pray that this year fruit will follow every seed you sow.

INHERITING THE PROMISES

SCRIPTURE OF THE WEEK

"And we desire that each one of you show the same diligence to the full assurance of hope until the end, that you do not become sluggish, but imitate those who through faith and patience inherit the promises." **Hebrews 6:11-12**

CONFESSION OF THE WEEK

- ᛦ I believe and confess that faithful is my God who has promised, He will surely bring all those things to pass in my life.
- ᛦ I decree that any tendency to stay content so much that I miss my next breakthrough is broken over my life in the name of Jesus.
- ᛦ I declare and decree as a child of God, that nothing will distract me from the path to the final

I believe and confess...

destination God has for me in the name of Jesus. I confess that I will not lose my focus in Jesus' name.

- I declare that no challenge shall cause me to turn back or stop on my way to my destiny. Every challenge that comes my way becomes a stepping stone for me to move to the next level in my life in Jesus' name.
- I believe and confess that as a child of God, I have not only started well but I will finish well too in the name of Jesus.
- From today, I will not stop at any stage on my way to the victorious destiny God has designed for me.
- I am blessed and highly favoured!

PRAYER POINTS FOR THE WEEK

- Pray and break over your life any tendency to stay content so much that you miss your next breakthrough the name of Jesus.
- Pray and destroy anything that is meant to distract you from the path to the final destination God has for you in the name of Jesus.

I believe and confess...

- Pray that you will not lose your focus no matter what comes your way in Jesus' name.
- Pray that the Lord will give you grace and strength that no challenge shall cause you to turn back or stop on your way to your destiny in Jesus' name
- Pray that from today, every challenge that comes your way becomes a stepping stone for you to move to the next level in your life in Jesus' name.

25th to 31st August

PARTAKING OF THE BLESSINGS

SCRIPTURE OF THE WEEK

"I will give you the treasures of darkness And hidden riches of secret places, that you may know that I, the Lord, Who call you by your name, Am the God of Israel." **Isaiah 45:3**

CONFESSION OF THE WEEK

- I believe and confess that silver and gold belongs to the Lord my God. As a child of God, I believe and confess that it is His will that I be rich and righteous.
- I declare and decree that I will not labour for others to reap in Jesus' name. I confess that I will not lie idle whilst others gather harvest.
- I believe and confess that I am rich and righteous and I will be a walking testimony.

I believe and confess...

- Harvest shall meet harvest in my life and I will leave an inheritance for my children's children.
- I confess that I will be a partaker of every blessing that God has destined for me and the blessing that God is bringing upon this nation will not pass me by.
- I declare that as I continue to honour God in my life my barns shall be filled with plenty and my vats shall overflow in the name of Jesus.
- I am blessed and highly favoured!

PRAYER POINTS FOR THE WEEK

- Pray in the name of Jesus that you will not labour for others to reap in Jesus' name.
- Pray that as you labour as directed by God, harvest shall meet harvest in your life and you will leave an inheritance for your children's children.
- Pray that together with household you will be partakers of every blessing that God has destined for your family.
- Pray that the blessing that God is bringing upon this nation will not pass you by in Jesus' name.

✝ Pray that as the Lord makes you a walking testimony you will still be rich and righteous and your life will continue to honour God in Jesus' name.

1st to 7th September

LOVE

SCRIPTURE OF THE WEEK

"A new commandment I give to you, that you love one another; as I have loved you, that you also love one another. By this all will know that you are My disciples, if you have love for one another." **John 13:34-35**

CONFESSION OF THE WEEK

- ༓ I believe and confess that my God is a merciful and loving God. By His great mercies and great love, He pulled me out of sin and made me His own through Christ Jesus.
- ༓ I declare that God has put in my heart the same love which He used to deliver me. I believe and confess that as a child of God, I will reach out and love those especially of the household of faith.

I believe and confess...

- ✥ I declare that as a member of the family of God, I will continually join my faith with others to see God do great exploits in our lives.
- ✥ I confess that the church of God will advance and do great exploits as we join together. I declare that, as a member of this family, God will use me to be a blessing to many in Jesus' name.
- ✥ I declare today that for the rest of my life, I will be an active member of the family of God.
- ✥ I am blessed and highly favoured!

PRAYER POINTS FOR THE WEEK

- ✥ Ask the Lord to put in your heart the same love which He used to deliver you.
- ✥ Pray for grace to reach out and love those especially of the household of faith even the unlovables.
- ✥ Pray that as a member of the family of God, you will continually join your faith with others to see God do great exploits in our lives.
- ✥ Pray that the church of God will advance and do great exploits as we join together.

I believe and confess...

✣ Pray that, as a member of this family, God will use you to be a blessing to many in Jesus' name.

8th to 14th September

POWER OF GOD

SCRIPTURE OF THE WEEK

"But you shall receive power when the Holy Spirit has come upon you; and you shall be witnesses to Me in Jerusalem, and in all Judea and Samaria, and to the end of the earth."
Acts 1:8

CONFESSION OF THE WEEK

- I believe and confess, that as a child of God, Jesus is my Lord and Saviour. I declare and decree that from today I receive an infilling of the Holy Spirit upon my life.
- My life is empowered in a new way in the name of Jesus. My spiritual life has taken a new dimension from today. Giftings and abilities are manifesting in my life right now in the name of Jesus.

I believe and confess...

- I declare and decree that the Spirit of God has come upon my life – to bring total transformation in my life.
- I declare and decree that the Spirit of God is causing me to do exploits that are beyond my natural strength and abilities in Jesus' name.
- I confess that from today I go out in the power of the Holy Spirit to be a witness for Christ.
- I declare and decree that from today I will break new grounds as I am empowered by the Holy Spirit in the name of Jesus.
- I believe and confess that I am blessed and highly favoured!

PRAYER POINTS FOR THE WEEK

- Pray that your life will be empowered in a new way in the name of Jesus.
- Pray that your spiritual life will take a new dimension from today and that giftings and abilities are manifesting in your life right now in the name of Jesus.

I believe and confess...

- Pray that the Spirit of God will come upon your life – to bring total transformation in your life.
- Pray that the Spirit of God will cause you to do exploits that are beyond your natural strength and abilities in Jesus name.
- Pray that as you go out in the power of the Holy Spirit to be a witness for Christ you will break new grounds and testimonies will follow in Jesus' name.

STAND UP AND BE COUNTED

SCRIPTURE OF THE WEEK

"For whoever is ashamed of Me and My words in this adulterous and sinful generation, of him the Son of Man also will be ashamed when He comes in the glory of His Father with the holy angels." **Mark 8:38**

CONFESSION OF THE WEEK

- ✤ I believe and confess that the Lord is my strength and my song. He has become my salvation.
- ✤ I declare that He is the rock on which I stand and I shall not be moved by challenges.
- ✤ I pray that the power and boldness of the Lord rest upon my life to make me a witness for God wherever I go in Jesus' Name.

I believe and confess...

- I declare and decree that wherever God places me, my life and work will glorify His name. I will not deny my God before anyone in Jesus' Name.
- I declare today that no temptation, no threat or compromise will cause me to disown my Lord in Jesus' name.
- I declare that from today I will use every position and opportunity God has blessed me with to further the kingdom of God. I will be an active member of the Lord's army in everything I do.
- I confess that from today I will stand up and be counted amongst those who are actively living for Christ.
- I am blessed and highly favoured!

PRAYER POINTS FOR THE WEEK

- Thank God for becoming your strength, your song and your salvation.
- Pray that the Lord will continue to be the rock on which you stand therefore you shall not be moved by challenges.

- Pray that the power and boldness of the Lord will continually rest upon your life to make you a witness for God wherever you go in Jesus' Name.
- Pray for divine enablement that wherever God places you, your life and work will glorify His name.
- Ask the Lord to give you grace to use every position and opportunity He has blessed you with to further the kingdom of God.

22nd to 28th September

BE A BLESSING

SCRIPTURE OF THE WEEK

"Be kindly affectionate to one another with brotherly love, in honor giving preference to one another." **Romans 12:10**

CONFESSION OF THE WEEK

- I believe and confess that the grace of God will make me grow in the likeness of Christ Jesus. I declare that as I receive the word of God, I will not remain the same but bear the fruit of the word.

- As a child of the Living God, I receive grace to walk by the direction of the Holy Spirit and not yield to the instructions of the flesh.

- I pray that God will make me a person who will be a blessing to those into whose life He brings me. I pray that the glory of God will be reflected in every area of my life.

I believe and confess...

- ✤ I believe and confess that my relationships will yield great testimonies. I confess that genuine peace and joy will abound in my home in the name of Jesus.
- ✤ I declare that from today, anger and bitterness will be far from me. The fruit of the spirit will manifest in my life and that kindness, goodness and faithfulness will be my portion in the name of Jesus.
- ✤ I am blessed and highly favoured!

PRAYER POINTS FOR THE WEEK

- ✤ Pray that the grace of God will make you grow in the likeness of Christ Jesus.
- ✤ Pray that as you continue to hear the word of God and do as it says that you will not remain the same but bear the fruit of the Word.
- ✤ Pray for the grace to walk by the direction of the Holy Spirit and not yield to the instructions of the flesh.
- ✤ Pray that God will make you a person who will be a blessing to those into whose life He brings you.

I believe and confess...

✥ Pray that all the days of your life the fruit of the spirit will manifest in your life.

29th September to 5th October

SERVING GOD

SCRIPTURE OF THE WEEK

"What shall I render to the Lord For all His benefits toward me? I will take up the cup of salvation, and call upon the name of the Lord. I will pay my vows to the Lord Now in the presence of all His people." **Psalms 116:12-14**

CONFESSION OF THE WEEK

- I believe and confess that it is by the goodness and mercies of God that I live. It is in Him that I live, I move and have my being.

- I thank the Lord that He paid the ultimate price for my salvation. As a child of God and a member of God's family, I declare that I will humble myself and reach out to be a blessing to those of the household of faith.

I believe and confess...

- I thank the Lord for the gifts, talents and abilities that He has blessed me with. I thank God for planting me in this family.
- I declare today that for the rest of my life, I will make myself available to be used of God in his house. I will not just be served but I make a decision today to serve God's people.
- I declare today that no offense shall rob me of the blessing associated with what I am assigned to do. I confess that I will remain focussed and serve gladly wherever I am needed.
- I believe and confess that my labour for the Lord will never ever be in vain, in Jesus' name.
- I am blessed and highly favoured!

PRAYER POINTS FOR THE WEEK

- Thank the Lord that He paid the ultimate price for your salvation.
- As a child of God and a member of God's family, I declare that I will humble myself and reach out to be a blessing to those of the household of faith.

I believe and confess...

- Pray for grace to make yourself available the rest of your life, to be used of God in His house.
- Pray that no offense shall rob you of the blessing associated with what you are assigned to do.
- Ask the Lord to help you remain focussed and serve gladly wherever you are needed.

6th to 12th October

TESTIMONY

SCRIPTURE OF THE WEEK

"And we know that all things work together for good to those who love God, to those who are the called according to His purpose." **Romans 8:28**

CONFESSION OF THE WEEK

- I believe and confess that the Lord God is in full control of my present and my future.
- I confess in the name of Jesus, that no mountain or storm will derail me from where God is taking me.
- I declare today that every problem that life throws at me, presents me with the perfect opportunity for God to release testimonies in my life.
- I declare today that the praise of the Lord will continually be in mouth. I will see signs and wonders in my life whilst I praise my Maker.

I believe and confess...

- As a child of God, as my prayers meets up with my praises to God every problem in my life will end up as a testimony in Jesus' name.
- I confess today that it is not over for me until God has the final word.
- I am blessed and highly favoured!

PRAYER POINTS FOR THE WEEK

- Pray in the name of Jesus that the Lord will take full control of your present and your future.
- Pray that no mountain or storm will derail you from where God is taking you.
- Pray that every problem that life has thrown at you God will use it a perfect opportunity to release testimonies in your life in Jesus' name.
- Pray that the enemy won't be able to take praise out of your mouth regardless of the challenge but the praise of the Lord will continually be in your mouth.
- Pray that as your prayers meet up with your praises to God every problem in your life will end up as a testimony in Jesus' name.

13th to 19th October

FINISHING WELL

SCRIPTURE OF THE WEEK

"Knowing this, that our old man was crucified with Him, that the body of sin might be done away with, that we should no longer be slaves of sin. For he who has died has been freed from sin." **Romans 6:6-7**

CONFESSION OF THE WEEK

- ꕥ I believe and confess that God has a purpose for my life and that purpose will manifest in the name of Jesus.

- ꕥ I decree today that I will not start in God's purpose for my life and fail to finish.

- ꕥ I declare and decree as a child of God, that no person, no scheme, no offer, no covenant will cause me to stray from where God has planted me

I believe and confess...

in the name of Jesus.

- I declare that the blessings that God has already given me will draw me closer to Him and not otherwise. I confess that I will promote the kingdom of God with the talents and giftings that God has given me.

- I believe and confess that as a child of God, I will never forget that God is my Source, my Helper and my Strength.

- From today, I declare that my eyes will be focussed on what God has in store for me. I will increase and excel in any assignment that God gives to me and my life will be a living testimony.

- I am blessed and highly favoured!

PRAYER POINTS FOR THE WEEK

- Pray that every purpose God has for your life will manifest in the name of Jesus.

- Pray in the name of Jesus that you will not start in God's purpose for your life and fail to finish; but you will finish well.

I believe and confess...

- ⚜ In the name of Jesus pray that no person, no scheme, no offer, no covenant will cause you to stray from where God has planted you.

- ⚜ Pray for grace not to be drawn away by the blessings that God has already given you but rather to draw me closer to Him.

- ⚜ Pray that from today, your eyes will be focussed on what God has in store for you and you will increase and excel in any assignment that He gives to you.

20th to 26th October

THE GLORY OF GOD

SCRIPTURE OF THE WEEK

"*Therefore whoever confesses Me before men, him I will also confess before My Father who is in heaven. But whoever denies Me before men, him I will also deny before My Father who is in heaven.*" **Matthew 10:32-33**

CONFESSION OF THE WEEK

- I believe and confess that Jesus is my Lord and personal Saviour. He has placed His glory upon every area of my life and I am a walking testimony.

- I declare that as a child of God, I offer myself as a living sacrifice, holy and acceptable to Him.

- I declare that from today, I will reflect His glory in my home. I will reflect His glory in my job. His glory will be seen in my way of doing business everywhere I go.

- I declare and decree that my personal commitment to living for God will not be in doubt to all around me and I will be passionate promoter of the kingdom of God in all my ways.

- I declare that God will bring more glory upon my life with signs and wonders following me in every area of my life.

- I declare today that for the rest of my life, I will live and stand for Christ.

- I am blessed and highly favoured!

PRAYER POINTS FOR THE WEEK

- Thank the Lord for placing His glory upon every area of your life and you are a walking testimony.

- Pray for grace to truly and fully offer yourself as a living sacrifice, holy and acceptable to Him.

- Pray that you will reflect the glory of God in your home, in your job and your way of doing business everywhere you go.

- Pray that your personal commitment to living for

I believe and confess...

God will not be in doubt to all around you and you will be passionate promoter of the kingdom of God in all my ways.

✥ Pray that the Lord will bring more glory upon your life with signs and wonders following you in every area of my life.

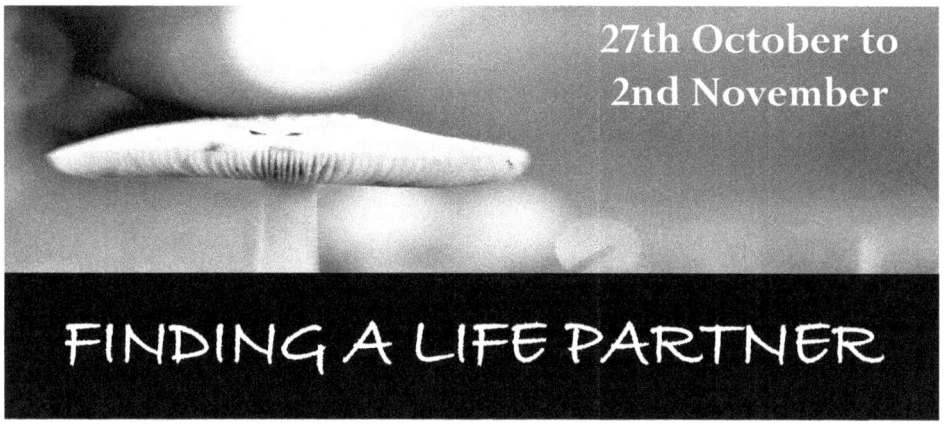

FINDING A LIFE PARTNER

SCRIPTURE OF THE WEEK

"He who finds a wife finds a good thing, And obtains favor from the Lord." **Proverbs 18:22**

CONFESSION OF THE WEEK

- ⚘ I believe and confess that the Lord is my strength and my guide. I declare that, as I seek, the Lord will direct my paths to find the person He has prepared for me.
- ⚘ And as I wait, I declare that any demonic veil that has covered my glory be removed in Jesus' name.
- ⚘ I pray that the Lord will deliver me from any Nabal and Delilah in my life. I confess that my future will not be compromised by any Nabal or Delilah in the name of Jesus.
- ⚘ From now on, I reject contention and strife in my

I believe and confess...

home in the name of Jesus. I declare that peace, joy and fruitfulness shall abide in my home in Jesus' name.

- I confess that the glory of the Lord will be made manifest in my life and home in the name of Jesus.
- I am blessed and highly favoured!

PRAYER POINTS FOR THE WEEK

- Pray that the Lord will direct your paths to find the person He has prepared for you.
- Pray that as you wait, any demonic veil that has covered your glory be removed in Jesus' name.
- Pray that the Lord will deliver you from any Nabal and Delilah in your life
- Pray that your future will not be compromised by any Nabal or Delilah in the name of Jesus.
- Pray that the glory of the Lord will be made manifest in your life and home in the name of Jesus.

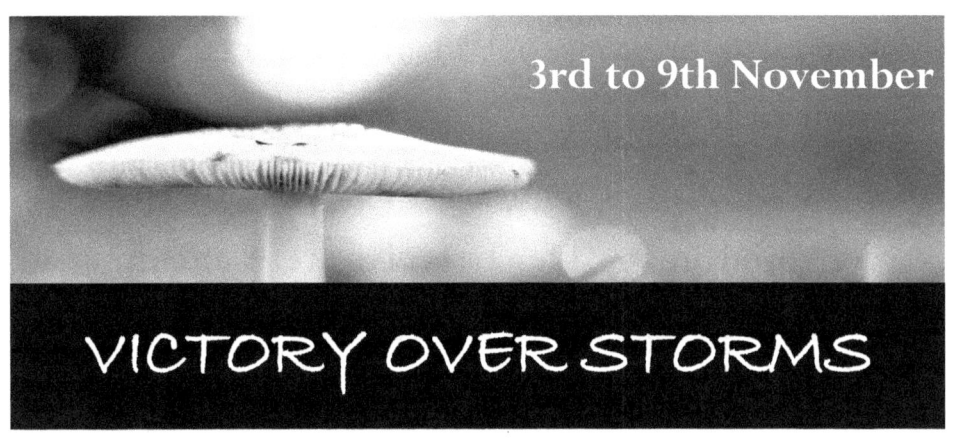

3rd to 9th November

VICTORY OVER STORMS

SCRIPTURE OF THE WEEK

"Hear my cry, O God; Attend to my prayer. From the end of the earth I will cry to You, when my heart is overwhelmed; Lead me to the rock that is higher than I." **Psalms 61:1-2**

CONFESSION OF THE WEEK

- I believe and confess that the Lord is my strength. I declare that the Lord will cause me to ride victoriously over every storm in the name of Jesus.
- I declare that the Lord will continue to be my source of refreshing all the days of my life. I pray that the Lord will uphold me when faced with challenges of life.
- I declare that from today the Lord is pouring out His spirit upon every area of my life. Revival is breaking out in my life in the name of Jesus.

I believe and confess...

Revival is breaking out in my local church in the name of Jesus.

- I confess that from today the spirit of apathy is destroyed in my life. I receive fresh anointing to break out of spiritual darkness.
- I break out of every hold of bitterness and pain that is holding me back in the name of Jesus.
- I confess that I am free from every hold of depression and I receive grace to grow from strength to strength and glory to glory.
- I am blessed and highly favoured!

PRAYER POINTS FOR THE WEEK

- Pray in the name of Jesus that the Lord will cause you to rise victoriously over every storm you are facing.
- Pray that you will break free from anything that is limiting your spiritual growth in the name of Jesus.
- Pray that the Lord will dispel any cloud of spiritual darkness hovering over your life.
- Pray and destroy any hold of anger and bitterness in your life.

I believe and confess...

- Pray and cast down any imagination that speaks against your God-given destiny

DESTROYING EVIL ASSOCIATIONS

SCRIPTURE OF THE WEEK

"Many sorrows shall be to the wicked; but he who trusts in the Lord, mercy shall surround him." **Psalms 32:10**

CONFESSION OF THE WEEK

- I believe and confess that the Lord will cause me to enter the destiny that He has prepared for me.
- I decree that from this day onwards I will walk in total victory over every destiny destroyer in Jesus' name. I declare that the Devil and his devices are under my feet in the name of Jesus.
- I declare that discontentment gives way to the joy of the Lord in my life in the name of Jesus. Worry and strife gives way to the peace of God that passes all understanding in the name of Jesus.
- I declare that as I anoint myself, may the unusual

peace follow me from this day onwards in Jesus name.

- I declare and decree that any wrong association sent to weaken me be exposed and destroyed in Jesus name. I declare today that any wrong association sent to wreck my business, career or ministry be stopped in Jesus' name.
- I declare today that the work of deception set against me will not prosper. Any work of darkness will be exposed in the name of Jesus. From today, may the light of God shine in every area of my life.
- I declare that from today I will not despise the house of God nor those God has put in spiritual authority over my life.
- I will not dishonour the family of God in the name of Jesus. I am thankful for the house where God has planted me.
- I am blessed and highly favoured!

PRAYER POINTS FOR THE WEEK

- Pray in the name of Jesus that the Lord will cause you to enter the destiny that He has prepared for you.

- Pray that you will walk in total victory over every destiny destroyer in Jesus' name.
- Pray that the Lord will expose any wrong association sent to weaken you in Jesus name.
- Pray and destroy any wrong association sent to wreck my business, marriage, career or ministry in the name of Jesus.
- Anoint yourself and pray that unusual peace and favour will follow you; doors will open by their own accord in Jesus name.

17th to 23rd November

ENCOURAGEMENT

SCRIPTURE OF THE WEEK

"The Lord upholds all who fall, and raises up all who are bowed down. The eyes of all look expectantly to You, and You give them their food in due season." **Psalms 145:14-15**

CONFESSION OF THE WEEK

- ✥ I believe and confess that I serve a living and faithful God. I serve a God whose word will never fail in my life.
- ✥ I confess today that the destiny that God has designed for my life will not remain a dream. It shall become reality in my life in Jesus' name.
- ✥ I declare and decree that from today I am a stranger to discontent. Discouragement will be far from me, and complaining will not be associated with me.

I believe and confess...

- I confess that the Lord will be my source of encouragement and I will be an encourager to my generation in the name of Jesus.
- I declare today that everything that God has designed for my life shall manifest as testimonies in my life. This week, I walk into a testimony in the name of Jesus.
- This week, I walk into good news in the name of Jesus. This week, I will experience new blessing in Jesus' name.
- I believe and confess that I am blessed and highly favoured.

PRAYER POINTS FOR THE WEEK

- Pray that the destiny that God has designed for your life will not remain a dream but it shall become reality in your life in Jesus' Name.
- Pray that from today will be stranger to discontentment, discouragement and complaining will be far from you in Jesus name.
- Pray that everything that God has designed for your life shall manifest as testimonies in your life.

I believe and confess...

- Pray that his week, you will receive good news from afar and near in the name of Jesus.
- Thank the Lord that He will continually be your source of encouragement.

24th to 30th November

SUBMISSION TO GOD

SCRIPTURE OF THE WEEK

"And you shall love the Lord your God with all your heart, with all your soul, with all your mind, and with all your strength.' This is the first commandment." **Mark 12:30**

CONFESSION OF THE WEEK

- I believe and confess that the Lord God is my Maker and in Him I live, in Him I move and have my being. He is my Rock and the pillar of my life – without Him I can do nothing.
- I confess that the grace of God will abound in my life that I will live a life that is totally submitted to Him.
- I yield my body, my soul, my mind and my spirit to the Almighty God and I declare that from today, I will put my all at God's disposal in the name of Jesus.

I believe and confess...

- I declare that I will use every part of my life for the promotion of God's kingdom. I will be the feet and mouth of the kingdom of God to reach souls for Christ.
- I will be the hands of the kingdom of God to serve God's people. I yield my talents and abilities to the Most High that He will use me to be a blessing to His people.
- I am blessed and highly favoured!

PRAYER POINTS FOR THE WEEK

- Pray that the grace of God will abound in your life.
- Pray that you will live a life that is totally submitted to God.
- Pray for creative ideas and grace to use every part of your life for the promotion of God's kingdom.
- Pray that the Lord will use you as His hands in the kingdom of God to serve God's people.
- Thank God for the privilege to be used to serve His people.

1st to 7th December

SUCCESS AND PROSPERITY

SCRIPTURE OF THE WEEK

"And you shall remember the Lord your God, for it is He who gives you power to get wealth, that He may establish His covenant which He swore to your fathers, as it is this day."
Deuteronomy 8:18

CONFESSION OF THE WEEK

- ❧ I believe and confess that the Lord is my source of success and prosperity. He gives me the wisdom and power to get wealth.
- ❧ I declare that I receive the spirit of diligence and excellence to create wealth. I receive the strength and wisdom to turn my gifts and talents to great wealth in Jesus' name.
- ❧ I confess that creative ideas begin to flow in my life now. I confess that agents of favour begin to arrive

I believe and confess...

- in my life in Jesus' name.
- I receive great wealth into my life to impact and change the lives of others. I declare and decree that from today I am a promoter of the kingdom of God in Jesus' name.
- By the wealth that God has given me, towns and cities shall hear and experience the word of God. By the wealth that God has given me, the kingdom of God will advance mightily and go beyond boundaries in Jesus' name.
- I am blessed and highly favoured!

PRAYER POINTS FOR THE WEEK

- Thank the Lord that He is your source of success and prosperity.
- Thank the Lord that He gives you the wisdom and power to get wealth.
- Pray that the Lord will give you the spirit of diligence and excellence to create wealth.
- Pray that the Lord will continue to give you strength and wisdom to turn your gifts and talents to great wealth in Jesus' name.

❧ Pray that by the wealth that God has given you, the kingdom of God will advance mightily and go beyond boundaries in Jesus' name.

8th to 14th December

INCREASE AND SATISFACTION

SCRIPTURE OF THE WEEK

"Thus says the Lord: 'Behold, I will bring back the captivity of Jacob's tents, and have mercy on his dwelling places; the city shall be built upon its own mound, and the palace shall remain according to its own plan. Then out of them shall proceed thanksgiving and the voice of those who make merry; I will multiply them, and they shall not diminish; I will also glorify them, and they shall not be small."

Jeremiah 30:18-19

CONFESSION OF THE WEEK

- I believe and confess that as I have waited on the Lord He will cause my light to break out from obscurity.

- My health is springing forth speedily in the name of Jesus. I declare that the Lord will guide me

I believe and confess...

continually and satisfy my soul even in drought.

- I confess that even in the time of drought, I shall be like a watered garden and I shall be fresh and flourishing.
- I declare and decree that from today, thanksgiving, joy and celebration shall break out in my life in the name of Jesus. A shout of joy shall be heard in my home in the name of Jesus.
- I declare that the Lord will prepare a table before me, even in the presence of my enemies. Those who have opposed me will be forced to rejoice with me.
- I decree that it is my time of celebration and I am blessed and highly favoured.

PRAYER POINTS FOR THE WEEK

- Pray that as you have waited on the Lord He will cause your light to break out from obscurity in Jesus name.
- Pray that your health will spring forth speedily in the name of Jesus.
- Pray that the Lord will guide you continually and

satisfy my soul even in drought in Jesus' name.

- Pray in the name of Jesus that regardless of the economic challenges and even in the time of drought, you shall be like a watered garden and you shall be fresh and flourishing.
- Pray that the Lord will prepare a table before you, even in the presence of your enemies

15th to 21st December

PRESENCE OF GOD

SCRIPTURE OF THE WEEK

"I will lift up my eyes to the hills-- From whence comes my help? My help comes from the Lord, Who made heaven and earth. He will not allow your foot to be moved; He who keeps you will not slumber." **Psalms 121:1-3**

CONFESSION OF THE WEEK

- ✤ I believe and confess that the Lord is my deliverer and my ever-present source of help.
- ✤ The presence and the mercies of God will be with me wherever I go in the name of Jesus.
- ✤ I declare as a child of God, that the Lord will never leave me nor forsake me.
- ✤ I declare that those who say there is no help for me will live to see the goodness of God manifest in my

I believe and confess...

life. Those who have set themselves against me will see the day of my deliverance.

- I declare that from today, I cease to rely on my earthly wisdom and strength to do exploits. My voice shall continually be heard in heaven as I seek the face of my God.

- I pray that the passion for prayer will never leave my life in the name of Jesus. May my desire to see God's will manifest in my life never be quenched.

- I declare today that for the rest of my life, I will not be a stranger at the throne of grace.

- I am blessed and highly favoured!

PRAYER POINTS FOR THE WEEK

- Pray that the presence and the mercies of God will be with you wherever you go in the name of Jesus.

- Thank God that He will never leave you nor forsake you.

- Pray that He will cause those who said there is no help for you to live to see the goodness of God manifest in your life in Jesus' name.

- Pray that the Lord will deliver you from those who have set themselves against you in Jesus' name.

- Pray that the passion for prayer will never leave your life in the name of Jesus and your desire to see God's will manifest in your life never be quenched.

THANKSGIVING

SCRIPTURE OF THE WEEK

"In everything give thanks; for this is the will of God in Christ Jesus for you." **1 Thessalonians 5:18**

CONFESSION OF THE WEEK

- I believe and confess that the praise of the Lord will continually be in my mouth.
- I thank my God for all that has happened in this year. I thank Him for the great victories and I thank Him for bringing me through the challenging storms.
- I declare today that even at this late stage of the year, I receive another testimony in my life in the name of Jesus.
- I confess today that the Lord will grant me a heart

I believe and confess...

of gratitude for the rest of my life.

- As a child of God, I declare that grumbling and complaints give way to thanksgiving in my life from now onwards.

- I am blessed and highly favoured!

PRAYER POINTS FOR THE WEEK

- Pray that the praise of the Lord will continually be in your mouth.

- Thank God for all that has happened in this year.

- Thank Him for the great victories.

- Thank Him for bringing you through the challenging storms.

- Pray that even at this late stage of the year, you shall receive another testimony in your life in the name of Jesus.

- Pray that the Lord will grant you a heart of gratitude for the rest of your life.

OTHER BOOKS BY THIS AUTHOR

FOREWORD BY MATTHEW ASHIMOLOWO

think before you wink

25 Questions You Should Be Answering During Courtship
13 Popular Myths About Sex
12 Guidelines For Stepping Up From A Broken Relationship

ANDY & HELEN YAWSON

Paperback and Kindle versions available on www.amazon.com or by email to illumination_house@yahoo.com

www.ingramcontent.com/pod-product-compliance
Lightning Source LLC
Chambersburg PA
CBHW061322040426
42444CB00011B/2729